Defeating
GANGS IN YOUR NEIGHBORHOOD AND ONLINE

PHILIP WOLNY

ROSEN
PUBLISHING®
New York

Published in 2016 by The Rosen Publishing Group, Inc.
29 East 21st Street, New York, NY 10010

First Edition

Library of Congress CataloginginPublication Data

Wolny, Philip.
 Defeating gangs in your neighborhood and online / Philip Wolny. -- First edition.
      pages cm. -- (Effective survival strategies)
 Includes bibliographical references and index.
 ISBN 978-1-4994-6151-0 (library bound)
 1. Gangs--United States--Juvenile literature. 2. Gang members--United States--Juvenile literature. 3. Juvenile delinquency--United States--Prevention--Juvenile literature. I. Title.
 HV6439.U5W66 2016
 364.106'60973--dc23
                                        2015022418

For many of the images in this book, the people photographed are models. The depictions do not imply actual situations or events.

Manufactured in China

Contents

4 INTRODUCTION

7 CHAPTER 1

WHAT ARE
GANGS?

16 CHAPTER 2

GANGS AROUND
YOU

26 CHAPTER 3

HOW TO AVOID
AND DEAL WITH
GANGS

34 CHAPTER 4

GANGS:
SOLUTIONS ON
THE GROUND

44 CHAPTER 5

FIGHTING BACK
AND THRIVING—
ONLINE AND OFF

54 GLOSSARY

55 FOR MORE INFORMATION

58 FOR FURTHER READING

59 BIBLIOGRAPHY

62 INDEX

Introduction

During the July 4th weekend in 2014, in Chicago, Illinois, there were eighty-two shootings. Fourteen of these were fatal. While violent and major crimes of all kinds have been on a decline in cities in recent years, Chicago, the third-largest city in the United States, has instead suffered an epidemic of gang violence, fueled by a boom in the illegal heroin trade. The number of violent incidents and gang-related murders has risen steadily in the past ten years and has renewed the city's reputation as a gang mecca.

Chicago is not alone. Many U.S. cities have troubling gang problems, including ones whose crime rates have otherwise declined, such as New York City. Some gang trouble spots include St. Louis, Missouri; Memphis, Tennessee; Oakland, California; and dozens of other mid-sized and large urban areas.

As *U.S. News* reported in March 2015, gangs are on the rise in the United States, even as overall violent crimes are reported to be decreasing. Senior researcher James Howell of the National Gang Center told *U.S. News* that, nationally, in the past five years, there has been "an 8 percent increase in the number of gangs, an 11 percent increase in members, and a 23 percent increase in gang-related homicides." He added that gangs were responsible for 16 percent of all killings and about a quarter of all homicides in cities with more than 100,000 people.

Gangs remain an unwelcome presence everywhere. They are known for problems ranging from minor juvenile delinquency to serious crimes like grand theft, drug trafficking, prostitution, and murder.

Street gangs remain a problem for youth and society at large, and not just in big cities. Middle-class suburbs and rural regions are also at risk. As living in big cities has become more expensive, poorer populations and people who have immigrated to the United States have been moving to the suburbs. Gangs have followed them and even spread to middle-class areas.

Gangs' presence online has expanded their reach. They now recruit for and promote their organizations, threaten each other and innocent bystanders, and organize their activities with a click on a smartphone or computer. Police have capitalized on this social media presence, but gang activity flies under their radar.

Ganglike activity such as bullying has also entered the Internet age. Young people now congregate online as much as they do at school or at the mall, and gangs can take their negative influence and intimidation 24-7. Cyberbullying is a widespread problem that previous generations had no experience with. Gangs can use these new tools to their advantage to pressure rivals and victims into silence.

Solutions and strategies to combat gangs exist, however, and can be found wherever concerned youth and their adult allies choose to cooperate. The Internet also offers many tools to power and amplify antigang efforts. Even just one person can make a difference—with a social network at his or her disposal, a person can connect with those who have similar ideas, and their efforts can double, even becoming unstoppable. In this resource, we will take a look at gangs and investigate ways to defeat them in your neighborhood and online.

CHAPTER 1

WHAT ARE GANGS?

When people speak of "gangs," what do they mean, exactly? There is no exact definition of the term, and people in different areas, whether they are teenagers, adults, politicians, or law enforcement, make their own definitions.

However, for purposes of this resource, and in most of the public imagination, the term "gang" is short for "street gang." A gang's main activities are in the street, in the community at large, at school, or in other public places. They are also different from other groups, including criminal organizations like crews of thieves, adult organized crime groups like the Mafia, prison gangs, or other outlaws, such as members of some motorcycle clubs. They also differ from organized crime groups that engage in activities such as identity theft, computer hacking, human trafficking, and other offenses. Street gangs sometimes have ties to such groups and are similar in their structures, but they are a distinct phenomenon.

While gang activity has long been identified with males, gangs in the twenty-first century have changed. Female membership in gangs has risen, and female roles in gangs have changed, too.

According to the National Gang Center, there are several characteristics of gangs. These often include the following:

A gang has three or more members.

Gangs are made up of adolescents, teenagers, and young people, usually between the ages of twelve and twenty-four.

A gang has an identity, usually tied to a name.

Gang members view each other and are recognized by outsiders as a gang.

Gangs are organized and have some "permanence"—that is, members stick around for a while.

Gangs take part in "elevated" criminal activity—everything from petty crime, including minor assaults, to more serious crimes.

Gang Members: Telltale Signs

Gang members bond and establish an identity, both among their peers and to the world at large. These can include physical symbols of gang affiliation such as clothes or tattoos, as well as actions, names, codes, and other identifiers.

The stereotype of gang members is that most are tough-looking or intimidating young men. Some gang members are tougher to spot, however. Because law enforcement has come down hard on gangs, greater secrecy and a lower profile can benefit gangs that are more interested in money than promoting fearsome reputations. Still, for most teens, financial motivations for gang activity are less important. The sense of belonging and identity are among the most important reasons. One big way of establishing identity is through personal appearance.

Gang Colors

Southern California–based gangs cultivated very specific clothing styles to signify their place in gang culture and to their particular gangs. One way is through similar or identical clothing or colors. The gangs of Los Angeles, such as the Bloods and Crips, for example, are identified with the colors blue and red, respectively. Gang photos often portray gang members sporting these color schemes in items such as baseball caps, bandanas,

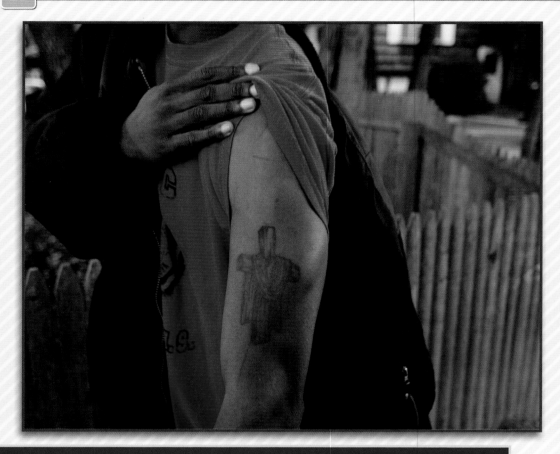

Gangs have steadily moved into America's suburbs. Here, a Blood wearing the gang's traditional red from Central Islip, a town in suburban New York's Suffolk County, flashes a tattoo.

T-shirts, socks, sneakers, and other clothing and accessories. Many Latino gangs in California often adopt a simpler style, with white T-shirts, thin belts, baggy pants or shorts, and bandanas.

There are many rituals surrounding the sporting of colors. Gangs may challenge others in public if they see people wearing rival colors, even if they are mistaken and they are not even really gang members. Gangsters might avoid sporting their colors if they are in a rival territory, too.

MAJOR CRIMES: THE DRUG GAME

Gang members may graduate from petty crime to more dangerous pursuits, including violent ones. These can include muggings, burglary, grand theft auto, and even bank robbery.

One of the most common—and often one of the most profitable—activities that gangs engage in to make money is dealing drugs. Established gangs control the narcotics trade because they have enough people—also known as "muscle"—and often the weaponry to protect their lucrative business.

To make more money, a gang must keep others from selling in the same area, thus eliminating competition. Because profits can run into the millions on drugs like cocaine, heroin, methamphetamine, marijuana, and many other illegal narcotics, the stakes are high. Gangs often maim and kill when they fear their interests are threatened. In many cases, their reputation and their business go hand in hand. They know that showing weakness in certain situations invites others to challenge them.

Tattoos and Gang Signs

Another indicator of gang membership is having a particular kind of tattoo. It is less of a true sign nowadays, of course, since tattooing has become a mainstream art form. Gang members may have more tattoos, or "ink," than the average person. A

This member of Mara Salvatrucha (or MS-13), a gang with thousands of members in the United States, was captured in El Salvador, where much of MS-13 has roots. His face tattoo signifies hardcore, lifelong membership.

"hardcore" gangster—someone who is totally committed to the lifestyle—may have facial tattoos.

Gang tattoos might depict illegal activity or symbols related to violence, death, and power, including skulls, crowns, weapons, cobwebs (often rumored to indicate someone has committed murder), and other illustrations. Members might place the gang's name in plain sight on their bodies or coded symbols and numbers. Members of the notoriously violent Mara Salvatrucha 13 gang, originally a Salvadorian gang, often sport a "13" somewhere on their body, written in regular numbers, Roman numerals, or a combination of the two.

Gangs are also distinguished by their use of gang signs. Some are self-evident; others are harder to translate. Displaying these is also known as "throwing up" gang signs and sometimes as "stacking." Signs are a way for members to identify or greet each other or warn and threaten rivals.

Where Does Gang Activity Occur?

Gangs can form wherever young people are. These include places like schools, the common areas of apartment complexes, parks, and other public places such as malls or even on public transportation. Their territory may be away from the unwelcome intrusions of adults, especially law enforcement, teachers, and administrators.

Gangs are most at home on the streets. They may or may not have regular meeting spots or even a headquarters or clubhouse. An abandoned building or the home of a member whose parents or guardians are never around may also serve as a headquarters.

A group of friends from the same school might form a gang. Other gangs draw their members from their immediate neighborhoods. They may stake a claim to a particular territory, or turf, for example, a particular set of buildings in a housing project, a specific street, or a park. If its primary illegal activity is selling drugs, it will violently defend its turf from competitors that threaten its livelihood.

What Gangs Do

Gangs vary widely in their activities, although there are many commonalities among them. One is members' willingness to use violence. They might fight to achieve a goal or dominate their rivals. Others fight out of general boredom and anger.

The media-fostered perception that competing over drug turf is a main driver of gang violence is incorrect. According to the National Gang Center's website, "In multiple studies over the past 25 years, a repeated finding is the lack of a drug component surrounding gang-related homicides." Conflicts over being disrespected are far more common. It is more likely that you will hear about a gang fight over someone losing face or after words are exchanged at a party than over contested drug turf.

Gangs also engage in many of the activities that normal teens do and may do so while mixing with non-gang members. This is often where tensions might occur, too, because it is up to the "normal" kids to be aware that they should tread carefully around

While some graffiti falls under the category of street art, much of gang graffiti is used primarily to mark territory and is amateurish and often ugly in appearance.

gangs. Along with actual members, many gangs have hangers-on around them that either hope to one day join the gang or gravitate to them because of drugs, alcohol, or some other perceived benefit.

Graffiti

Another common crime, and one that arises out of the gangs trying to make others respect and fear their reputations, is vandalism—specifically in the form of graffiti. While graffiti crews do exist and may be mistaken for gangs, these types of crews are usually organized primarily for the sake of their art and a renegade kind of thrill seeking.

Gang graffiti is different, however. It can be used to mark a gang's hangouts and map out their territory. It can also be used to start and escalate beefs between rivals. A common way to disrespect a rival gang member or gang, and thus provoke a confrontation, is to cross out the written name, or tag, of that member or the gang itself. A conflict that unfolds on marked-up walls can easily turn into physical altercations.

CHAPTER 2

GANGS AROUND YOU

Gangs are considered a major problem for society at large. For young people, gangs are more than an abstract idea, however. Whatever they call themselves—whether a gang, crew, set, or posse—they can be a very real and daily pitfall of a young person's life.

The presence of gangs in your school or neighborhood might be subtle, or it could be explicit. You may or may not interact directly with gangs, but you may see the effects of their presence. This might include innocuous evidence, like graffiti.

Gang activity might be more serious, however. Members might pick fights with you or your friends. They can attract negative attention from rivals and put others in danger as a result. School and after-school activities can be disrupted or made unsafe for normal students.

Teens' quality of life suffers wherever gang tensions and violence escalate. Teens can suffer as much from the stress of having to avoid and deal with gangs as they do with other

Law enforcement officers check the tattoos and identification of a suspected gang member. Real gangs are often targets of the authorities, and gang-afflicted areas are thus heavily policed.

negative aspects of their environment. It is in everybody's best interest—both in and out of gangs—that the gang problem is dealt with.

Why Do Gangs Form?

It is one thing to identify the threat of gangs in your area, but it's not so easy to figure out the underlying causes of them taking root. Understanding these origins and causes can help you and others team up to do something about them. Turning a critical eye toward yourself, you can also ask if you or your family members or friends could possibly be ensnared by the gang lifestyle.

Tough Neighborhoods, Tough People

While gang activity exists throughout all strata of society, the most fertile ground for gangs to take root is among poor and working-class youth, whether in urban or suburban settings. Millions of U.S. families are segregated in depressed areas like slums and public housing, with high unemployment, dysfunctional schools, and troubled family life all contributing to swelling gang membership.

The poor in communities of color are often incarcerated at much higher rates than white Americans. They are also fined excessively for minor infractions and constantly deal with overaggressive law enforcement. Even young children may be constantly followed and harassed by the authorities, while policies like New York's "stop-and-frisk" program have been decried as anything but random. A population that feels neglected and is constantly portrayed in the media and by teachers and social services as worthless or lacking fuels much resentment.

Young people who resent the power structure—whether it be the police, their schools, or just adults in general—might be drawn to a culture that scorns legality. Gang membership gives a sense of power to many who otherwise feel powerless.

Of course, there are alternatives to gangs when it comes to reclaiming some agency in the face of an unfair system. People volunteer with nonprofits, churches, or other organizations and wage campaigns for social justice. They mentor or befriend younger protégés and find constructive ways to make the world a better place. It is always important to remember that even if the world seems unfair, there are many others out there fighting to even the playing field for everyone.

Self-Esteem and Belonging

Lacking opportunities and role models, the gang lifestyle offers young men—and many young women now, too—a sense of belonging, self-esteem, and the esteem of others. When the "American dream" is nearly impossible to grasp, much less achieve, joining a gang offers the validation and even a sense of family for those who find these things are missing from their lives. They find structure they can embrace within a gang.

For others, joining a gang is like joining a family business, especially if one's older siblings or parents have been gang members. It may be more difficult not to join the gang lifestyle and walk away to find an alternative. With certain gangs in places like

There are many motivations that drive young people to gang membership. One of these is distrust of society's institutions, authorities, parents, and educators, a divide that results in an "us vs. them" mentality.

Chicago and Los Angeles having existed since the 1970s, there are even third-generation gang members of age now. Like growing up in war or being brought up in any chaotic environment, a legacy of gang involvement can be difficult to shake.

The Appeal of Gangs

The United States Department of Justice (DOJ), in its 2010 *Juvenile Justice Bulletin*, outlined some major motivations to join gangs, largely from the gang members' own point of view. Despite a public perception that many teens are forced into gangs somehow, the bulletin reports, "Most youth who join want to belong to a gang. Gangs are often at the center of appealing social action—parties, hanging out, music, drugs, and opportunities to socialize with the members of the opposite sex."

The DOJ report went on to list the following reasons preteens and teens join gangs in order from more important to less: for protection; for fun or to avoid boredom; for respect; for money; and to be like one or more of their friends.

Economic Motivations

Gang violence and homicides may not arise primarily out of the drug trade, but many gangs are involved in narcotics in some manner, some more extensively than others. In disadvantaged urban areas, the drug trade is the most profitable business to be in, and the lure of easy money is strong.

In some cases, gangs may arise and recruit more members if they start or expand a drug enterprise. Gangs that deal drugs or are involved in more serious crimes are often more secretive and strict. They are also more likely to be armed with weapons,

The high demand for illegal narcotics throughout all sectors of society makes drug dealing a lucrative moneymaking opportunity for many gangs. It is especially appealing in a time of high teen unemployment.

especially firearms, and ready to employ violence to protect their interests and members from competition, rivals, and law enforcement.

Social Pressures

Every teenager or preteen knows that this stage of one's life is fraught with uncertainty, insecurity, trying to figure out how to socialize, and how to deal with growing up. It can be tough enough negotiating normal peer groups and cliques.

The stakes are higher when gangs lurk on the social scene. Your friends may gravitate toward the gang. To keep these friends, you may be tempted to as well. Being around gangs can make for uncomfortable and nerve-racking surroundings.

In rough areas, youth also join gangs for security and protection. Unaffiliated, independent youth might feel vulnerable and thus seek out gangs. Fear of being victimized is valid and understandable. The motivation of seeking "respect" is tied to security. If someone is respected, it often means that others will not try to victimize him or her.

People who join a gang for protection, or have thought about it, must realize that they are likely giving up as much security in their daily life as they are supposedly gaining. They may avoid being bullied occasionally. But they are making themselves vulnerable to threats from rivals.

Once part of a gang, you cannot pick and choose your battles. To remain in good standing, you will always have to step up and defend the gang and all its members. If you are lucky, this may mean a few scuffles here and there. With worse luck, you could get badly beaten, shot, stabbed, and even killed. Are you prepared for such an unpredictable lifestyle?

Many American suburbs can be alienating places with little in the way of recreation or activities, including a lack of facilities and attractions that can draw teens' interest. The same may be true of certain rural areas. In these cases, sheer boredom may drive young people to petty crime and minor forms of juvenile delinquency. These can easily snowball into recreational drug use and more criminal behavior, including gang formation.

GANGS: WHERE THE GIRLS ARE

Are girls joining gangs more than ever before? The National Gang Center reports that exact numbers are inconclusive. Law enforcement agencies report female membership in gangs has remained stable since 2000 and has peaked at 7.7 percent nationally. However, other researchers believe that females might make up as much as 30 percent of gang membership, depending on the criteria researchers use.

It was once believed that most female gang members were female companions of male members. News stories in recent years seem to suggest that the nature of girls' roles in gangs may have changed. These days, there are more reports of gangs forming or branching out into all-female subsets, or cliques. Reports from gang hotbeds such as Chicago and New York City report that more girls are being prosecuted for scuffles, stabbings, and more serious violent acts. Other roles for females in gangs include hiding or holding weapons or drugs and even serving as "bait" to lure rival male gang members to parties to be attacked, according to one *NY Post* report on female gang members in New York's Harlem in 2010.

Girls can be especially vulnerable while living the gang lifestyle. Rival gangs and their own fellow gang members might victimize them in various ways. Girls might be endangered in situations such as parties where alcohol and drugs are plentiful. They are more prone to sexual assault.

Even worse, many female runaways and escapees from broken homes may seek the company of gangs for

(continued on the next page)

(continued from previous page)

A teenager wears clothing that is sometimes identified with the cholo and chola subculture of Southern California, including a plaid shirt buttoned up at the top. Some authorities consider this a gang uniform among Mexican American youth.

protection from the streets and can end up the "sexual property" of these groups. According to a 2009 report by the Chicago Alliance Against Sexual Exploitation (CAASE), of 1.5 million runaways in the United States, about one-third have engaged in prostitution. Gangs often exploit young girls because selling them for sex is easier than making money from drugs and far harder to prosecute.

Signs That Someone You Know Has Joined a Gang

You may be worried that someone you know—a friend, perhaps even a cousin or sibling—is contemplating joining a gang or has already done so. Beyond normal teenage angst and acting out, certain signs may point to gang membership.

These might include a change in the crowd someone normally hangs out with. The person may start acting strangely and being unusually secretive about his or her plans, activities, and whereabouts. The person might suddenly have money, and it did not come from his or her parents or from working a job.

A person might also exhibit some of the physical clues already discussed, including flashing hand signs and the tendency to repeatedly wear the same color combination. A formerly sober student might show symptoms of substance abuse. The appearance of a new tattoo, either real or even self-drawn with ink, can also be an indicator.

CHAPTER 3

HOW TO AVOID AND DEAL WITH GANGS

Dealing with gangs around you, whether in your social circles or your neighborhood or online, takes awareness, intelligence, compassion, and confidence.

Choosing Friends Wisely

If you just moved from somewhere or are entering a new school, it can be both scary and exciting to work from a blank slate. It makes all the difference what friends you pick and what friends pick you. It is easy to fall in with the wrong crowd early on if you are not careful. Those who fall under the sway of gangs often have low self-esteem and thus crave the acceptance, anonymity, and power of a group.

Summoning forth your own individuality and confidence will keep you from befriending those who just want to take advantage

While it may be difficult in some schools and neighborhoods and may make you feel left out, going your own way often shows more courage and individuality than conforming to the gang lifestyle.

of you or who may only offer toxic friendships. If you are asked to do anything criminal or engage in bullying or violence against anyone, think about it seriously: do you feel good about this, deep down? Making your own decisions makes you a leader rather than a follower.

Reputation and Flash: Only Skin-Deep

Those that join gangs for the glory, excitement, or status are often disappointed. The rumors of earning lots of easy money, fighting for a cause, and camaraderie are attractive, but the reality often falls short. Gang members are more likely to get injured or worse and become disillusioned with the actual daily grind of gang life. Earning big money is out of reach for most young, low-level gang members.

Some may sport flashy clothing, new sneakers, and jewelry, but they are often broke most of the time. A reputation is often all a gang member truly has, and many will pretend, or "front," to maintain that reputation. Knowing this will help you and others avoid one of the lures of gang life.

Sometimes, the only way to stand up to a dangerous gang and escape harm is to report their activities to the police anonymously. This is especially true if an anonymous tipster fears for his or her loved ones' safety.

Informing on or Reporting Gangs to the Authorities

There have been many debates on whether individuals should act anonymously to inform on gang activity. These programs can be helpful, but they are problematic because an anonymous tipster can inform on anyone he or she chooses and may sometimes do so out of mere self-interest—for example, to claim a cash award or to get back at someone else, and not out of the goodness of his or her heart.

Some people in urban areas have embraced the "Stop Snitching" movement. Because of the very real and troubled history African American communities have had with law enforcement, many have pledged not to inform the police about criminal activity. This is because they have felt over-policed. However, these attitudes have also prevented many people from coming forward with information on gang violence they may have heard about or witnessed personally, including serious crimes like murder.

Standing Up Publicly

Confronting a gang openly is also a dangerous and unpredictable option. Reality is nothing like the typical Hollywood action film, where a courageous hero stands up to bullies or gangs and vanquishes them.

However, those who are being bullied or otherwise have suffered violence or harassment from a gang need to protect themselves. This may involve publicly filing a complaint or having police arrest a gang member. Depending on a gang's notoriety and history of violence, it may be necessary to make arrangements to protect yourself. You may want to seek out school counselors, school safety officers, or even other community leaders and volunteers to best figure out how to keep yourself safe.

Responding with Violence

In real life, members of gangs are people, too. Many are troubled and come from difficult upbringings. They embrace gang life to fill a hole in themselves. To preserve your well-being and that of a fellow human being, it is always best to avoid violence.

PROTECT YOURSELF— LEGALLY

Standing up to gang activity also means protecting yourself from the fallout of your actions. It may seem far-fetched, but being swept up by police or other official actions (such as school disciplinary measures) is not unheard of, even for those who innocently want to help. Depending on how close you are to gang members, you must make sure that any information cannot be misunderstood as self-incriminating and later used against you, even if it only mistakenly discredits you.

Enlist the aid of someone you can trust to advocate for you in "the system": perhaps a parent, guardian, adult relative, favorite teacher, counselor, or clergy member. If you can afford it or can find it cheap or free, you should seek legal counsel—in other words, it is advisable to hire a lawyer. The last thing an innocent bystander needs is to be blamed for the crimes of others.

In addition, since gang members are more experienced with fighting than you are, you are likely to get hurt yourself. You might also hurt someone badly enough that you yourself may be prosecuted for a crime. Poorly planned acts of retribution can end up hurting innocent bystanders, too.

This is not to say that you should not defend yourself if you are attacked. Living in a tough environment can mean that a personal attack is a possibility. Taking self-defense classes, wrestling, and getting other training, such as at a martial arts academy, are ways to keep confident in the event that you are forced to defend yourself.

Violence, even in self-defense, should be a last resort, however. It is always best to walk away from conflict, especially if weapons may be involved. In the heat of the moment, it is likely you may not think your actions through properly and overestimate your own strength or abilities. Always think of your safety and health—both mental and physical—and of those around you.

Giving In to Gangs

One attitude you might have is the classic "If you can't beat them, join them." It is easier to cave in to this option if you have no clue what a potentially tough path lies ahead as a gang member.

Ways of joining a gang differ. One troubling part of some gang initiations involves being "jumped in"—this means that several established gang members assault you, either by hand or even with weapons. Another common initiation method is for the new person to commit a crime. This may include stealing something or even assaulting a stranger, for example. You thus risk injury, criminal prosecution, and even seriously maiming or even killing someone accidentally.

When it seems that gang presence confronts you at every turn—for example, at school, where you spend so much time—it may feel easier to give in than to stand strong. Think hard, however, before caving in.

With other groups, it may be easier to join a gang, with little more necessary than being recommended by another member or being a part of a legacy because an older sibling or family member belongs to the gang.

However hard it is to get in, it may be even more difficult to retire or leave the lifestyle behind. Depending on how hardcore a group is, they may not look kindly upon someone leaving. They may fear that this person may betray them to other gangs or may inform or snitch on them to the authorities. Some gangs might threaten quitters with violence. More dangerous groups sometimes even kill members who have strayed from what most of the gang members see as a lifetime commitment.

A Bleak Future

Ultimately, the risks one takes in joining a gang far outweigh the potential benefits. Gang life is no substitute for a life, career, or any other positive pursuit. Being in one is a young person's game. Members risk wasting years of their lives fighting, dealing drugs, and possibly even in prison. Many gang members who leave the life later on find they have few employment prospects because they lack even a high school diploma or basic job skills, and a criminal record means even fewer opportunities. They can end up feeling hopeless in their thirties and forties, a time when others are beginning to hit their stride.

CHAPTER 4

GANGS: SOLUTIONS ON THE GROUND

Some may feel that the solutions to gang activity in any one area might lie in more effective law enforcement strategies, but many communities have learned that a balanced approach may work as well or better. Policing, especially when it comes to catching and jailing dangerous and violent offenders, can be an important component of any antigang campaign. If you feel threatened and fear for your health and even your life, going to the police may be the only choice you have.

However, to truly make an impact on gangs, a combination of measures may be necessary. No one has yet discovered the cure-all, and gang activity has seemed to rise steadily, despite stricter policing. Still, the symptoms of the gang lifestyle can be alleviated and curbed, and there are many options besides the law-and-order approach.

Police and gangs are often perceived to be in conflict with each other. However, in recent years, there has been a shift in some people's thinking to embrace dialogue and nonpunitive youth intervention to address gang problems.

The Police vs. Gangs

We often think of law enforcement and gangs at odds with each other. However, it is sometimes police officers that have the closest familiarity and contact with gang members, their families, and environments. This intimate knowledge leaves police uniquely positioned to intervene in the lives of many troubled youth.

Suppression

Police intervention in the gang problem can take several forms. The most familiar is through "suppression." Suppression efforts concentrate on harshly punishing gangs and their members.

Many people point out that heavy police suppression can have the opposite effect than intended: it can give gangs more resolve to rebel against society and the system, fostering an "us vs. them" mentality. Suppression also casts a wide net and often ensnares non-gang members, too. It makes community-police relations tense and often results in the kind of harsh policing that angers communities, leading community members to feel that they are occupied by police rather than protected.

Zero Tolerance: The School-to-Prison Pipeline

Valuing security and safety above all else can make even sensible people overreact and make problems seem bigger than they are. One example has been zero tolerance policies in schools. These became popular in the 1990s after a series of school shootings, including the Columbine massacre. A series of panics over drugs and gang activity in schools also made many school administrators, parents, and police embrace these measures.

Zero tolerance policies penalize even minor infractions with harsh penalties. Many juveniles, and even children in junior high school and elementary grades, have been suspended, expelled, and even jailed for offenses as minor as talking loud in class, drawing a picture of a gun, throwing tantrums, or even simply horsing around with friends.

Such policies disproportionately target children of color and disadvantaged students in general. These minor offenses have left thousands of children nationwide with permanent disciplinary records, and even criminal records, which alienate youth and often push students into criminal behavior. This is a phenomenon known as the "school-to-prison pipeline." Meanwhile, teachers

It is easier these days, fairly or not, to be labeled a gang member. Staying out of trouble is the easiest way not to get mixed up in activities that could get you sucked into the juvenile justice and prison systems.

and administrators turned over what used to be disciplinary matters handled by schools themselves to the harsher discipline of law enforcement.

In this climate, it is not hard to see how a regular group of friends in a high school, who may favor certain types of clothes or music—whether hardcore rap or heavy metal—and may misbehave or rebel, can easily be mislabeled as a gang. Many law enforcement observers and scholars point out that zero tolerance and suppression policies have largely failed to curb gang culture. Gangs have only become more widespread since such policies have proliferated.

Everyone's a VIP

Many law enforcement officials and agents are turning to non-punitive intervention tactics. Some of those trying to curb gang activity are turning away from incarceration and imposing monetary fines, opting instead for more compassionate intervention. The *Star Tribune* reported in October 2013 about the Violence Intervention and Prevention (VIP) project in St. Paul, Minnesota. VIP was launched to both reduce punishment of juveniles and young people and connect them to social services so that they can avoid street life—and street crime. It ultimately cut serious crimes committed by youth by 20 percent.

For many teens, getting help can be a problem because they don't even know that there are resources to help them or how to access them. Services for teens are scattered among different agencies, and finding out about them can be difficult. Some municipalities (city governments) have tried to address this problem by creating one-stop shops for teens to get help with schoolwork, dealing with family issues, and applying for emergency aid, such as medical resources, free meals, and other needs. These are bundled with other services, like job counseling, tutoring, psychological counseling or therapy, and other needs for at-risk youth.

Many troubled youth simply need to know that someone cares. This is especially true if they come from troubled and/or abusive environments and have few or no adults they can look up to or trust. If adults have neglected them throughout their lives, a dedicated and caring authority figure who goes out of his or her way to listen or help can make all the difference.

Prevention and Alternative Approaches

Prevention and more hands-on approaches, including community policing, are alternatives and may even be used in conjunction with law-and-order approaches. Many approaches simply incorporate talking to at-risk youth or active gang members and encouraging them to get out or to avoid recruitment in the first place.

The Gang Resistance and Education and Training (GREAT) program recruits law enforcement officers to come to schools and present lectures and take questions from students all over the United States. They also team up with organizations like the Boys & Girls Clubs of America and the National Association of Police Athletics/Activities Leagues (PAL).

In turn, PAL programs also recruit police to coach youth sports and help children and teens with their homework and other school activities. Their aim is to help kids select alternative activities to hanging out on the street and to enrich youth and instill teamwork and leadership abilities. Boys & Girls Clubs Gang Prevention Through Targeted Outreach takes a similar approach and offers both school-related and social activities as alternatives to gangs, mainly through a large network of after-school programs in cities nationwide.

Some initiatives target kids long before they are "of age" to hang out with gangs. Programs serving boys seven to nine, such as Montreal's Preventive Treatment Program, offer parental guidance and skill training to children who have shown disruptive

THE INTERRUPTERS: ON THE FRONT LINES

Chicago, one of the nation's most gang-ridden cities, was the setting for a powerful and important 2011 documentary. In *The Interrupters*, filmmaker Steve James captured the stories of the volunteers of CeaseFire. CeaseFire is a grassroots group that is part of the larger Cure Violence organization. Its workers defuse and physically interrupt gang violence before and even as it happens.

The members of CeaseFire—also known as Interrupters—are all ex-convicts and gang members, and many were formerly incarcerated for violent offenses, some even for murder. Many come from the same communities where they now work. They build trust with active gang members using their own connections and forge new ones with the gang, even with some gang leaders.

Their greatest weapon is their credibility as wise veterans of the lifestyle, while their greatest obstacle is a culture of violence among the teens they are trying desperately to assist. The film tracks the progress of **the Interrupters** as they try to prevent youth from going down the same perilous road to ruin they themselves traveled.

For teens who prefer more informal organizations or methods to combat gang violence in their areas, groups like CeaseFire might be a great option. Even if you do not want to be right on the "front lines" talking down two crews who are escalating a beef, CeaseFire has a public education program that teens can get involved with. There are many ways to get involved, to help, and to be helped.

behavior as early as kindergarten. Though this was not specifically developed to prevent gang violence, it was actually shown
to do just that in the long term.

According to a DOJ report, in Brooklyn, Aggression
Replacement Training (ART), a program that helps prevent aggression and delinquency among adolescents, was also claimed by
administrators to have an effect. It concentrated on skills, along
with anger management and moral reasoning training.

Take the Initiative

Finding out if your area has similar programs available is as
simple as going online or approaching someone at your school.
Social services representatives from the city or state might also
be points of contact. If no one has visited your school to talk
about gangs, why not try to make it happen yourself? You may
even volunteer to help with implementation, which can give you
valuable experience organizing a nonprofit project.

Older gang members may be hard to reach. Some teens find
they can be mentors to younger children and adolescents and
influence them away from gang life. Children in elementary or
junior high school, especially those without good role models
who may already be acting out, can benefit greatly from one-on-
one attention from an older mentor. You need not be a successful
athlete or other overachiever to impact someone positively. You
only need to care. Consider talking to friends and even school
and community leaders to get a mentoring program in motion. It
can be tied into activities you and your friends already engage in,
such as sports, a book club, school theater, music, and anything
else you can imagine.

Pop Culture: Cultural Mirror or Glorifying Gangs?

Rap music began as a do-it-yourself music industry and was part of the original hip-hop culture. In the decades since it arose, it has become perhaps the most important popular culture of its era. While there are dozens of different styles and genres of rap, one of the most popular and commercially successful has been gangsta rap.

Rapper, actor, and television personality Ice-T is a pioneering hardcore hip-hop artist. He attended Crenshaw High School in South Los Angeles during a time of high gang activity, and his environment is frequently portrayed in his music.

Original gangsta rappers from the 1980s such as N.W.A. and Ice-T included extensive social commentary in their tracks. Chuck D, lead MC from the political rap act Public Enemy, once called rap music "Black America's CNN."

On the other hand, members of the society at large, including even older African Americans, have decried gangsta rap for its glorification of violence and the drug trade and for frequent and rampant misogyny. Those who know little about the hip-hop culture or about rap music are often these art forms' greatest critics. Some even deny that rap is music at all.

Gangsta rap is accused of glorifying gang life, drug dealing, misogyny, and violence. There are valid points to these criticisms. Rappers and fans often counter that heavy metal, pop, country, and other genres of music in which irresponsible behavior is glorified are rarely criticized as harshly. They feel that is because rap is perceived as "black music" and thus dangerous because of the race of the artists who create it.

To better deal with gangs, it is necessary to think critically and use common sense. Learn to distinguish between truly violent criminals versus those who are imitating a trend or simply living a fantasy they witness in music videos or online. A school administrator or older person might not successfully distinguish a regular teenager with tattoos and a hoodie from a gangbanger. Or he or she may even mistake a group of friends who simply dress similarly as members of a gang. In such cases, youth can help educate adults and each other and prioritize where to target their antigang efforts.

CHAPTER 5

FIGHTING BACK AND THRIVING— ONLINE AND OFF

No technology is all good or all bad. Just as gangs have expanded their reach in places like schools and neighborhoods, they may also congregate where most youth now gather—online.

Gangs—and Bullies—Online

Gang members have used the Internet to broadcast their interests, organize activities, and communicate. Online, they are able to plan and organize without having to meet physically. It is also just as easy to run afoul of gangs online and perhaps harder to avoid doing so.

It was once possible to leave school at 3 p.m. and get home having avoided the worst dangers of the street and feel safe. Modern youth do not have it so easy, however. Threats, bullying, and other forms of abuse can follow them home, via hurtful texts, instant messages, and people posting abusive or inappropriate messages on their social media profiles. Girls and LGBTQ

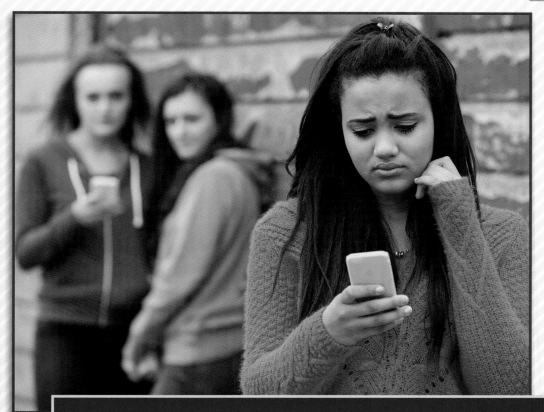

Whether you are dealing with gangs or cyberbullies, attacks and harassment delivered online or via smartphone can be as unsettling as dealing with it in person and can cause depression and even trauma.

(lesbian, gay, bisexual, transgender, and questioning) students are often particularly vulnerable, but those who stand up against gangs can also be easily targeted.

If you or a friend is being cyberbullied, it is important not to underestimate the seriousness of the harassers' actions. The stress and trauma from cyberbullying can sometimes have a greater affect on one's life than physical bruises. Dare to stand by friends when you can against cyberbullies, or, if necessary, enlist the help of adults. No one deserves to be harassed every-where he or she turns, 24-7.

PERFECT PEACE MINISTRY YOUTH OUTREACH: A PROFILE IN GANG INTERVENTION

Pastor Vernon Williams of Perfect Peace Ministry Youth Outreach, told AllThingsHarlem.com in 2010 about how New York City's Harlem neighborhood was facing the gang problem. Williams estimated in 2010 that there were about thirty active gangs in Harlem.

Williams himself has credibility on Harlem's streets. As a young man, he lived a life of violence and drug-dealing himself. He was imprisoned several times on various charges, and his longest stint in jail was a six-year sentence. It was during his last incarceration that he began to study the Bible.

He eventually became a preacher, and since then he has specialized in trying to prevent gang members from escalating tense situations. This often involves him driving around Harlem and personally breaking up some fights and preventing others. Williams has waded into potential shooting situations and has risked his life more than once.

Williams's organization, the Perfect Peace Ministry, also does online what he and some of his associates do in person. Volunteers familiar with the community help Williams scour social media sites like Facebook, Twitter, and other networks to monitor the Internet usage of more than four thousand at-risk teens. They engage directly in comments and send messages in situations where they think Internet arguments among potential gang members might be getting out of hand.

In other cases, monitoring tweets and other messages allows ministry volunteers to pinpoint crises and send their staff out to intervene. Williams told the *New York Daily News* about one particular beef in Harlem in November 2009. "They were threatening to go out and hurt two people," Williams said of one gang, the Get Money Boys, who had exchanged words online with the Goodfellas and the New Dons, two rival Harlem gangs. These exchanges allowed his staff to go out and target the gangsters in person, to try and talk them down from the conflict.

While professional antigang workers are on the front lines, everyone and anyone can contribute to solutions. Teens themselves, because they are closest to at-risk youth who may be their friends, siblings, and neighbors, are in a unique position to help others and raise awareness in their communities. In other words, be the change you want to see when it comes to defeating gangs. More and more, going online offers logistical and strategic ways to do just that.

A Golden Era for Online Organizing

Before the era of the Internet and mobile phones, imagine the amount of organization and effort needed to get the word out to solve a problem or organize a group of people to do something about gangs, for example. It required phone calls that might not be answered right away, going door to door, trying to solicit help in public, or enlisting people in person at school. Making fliers, writing letters, and informing important people about an anti-gang measure or project could take a lot of effort and cost a bit of money, for little or uncertain returns.

Despite cyberbullying and other pitfalls online, the Internet also empowers young people and multiplies their efforts via social media and powerful software and applications. Technology makes it even easier for one person to make a difference.

Nowadays, the ease of communication and connection the Internet offers has greatly reduced the effort required to push a plan forward. One person can easily enlist another, and a third, and each new recruit can expand a plan's reach many times over.

It has also made organizing much cheaper, too. For little or no money and minimal effort, you can organize a meeting, rally, march, or other awareness-raising event for your cause.

A Wealth of Platforms and Apps

There are many Internet platforms, online applications, and social networks available nowadays to achieve your goals. Online resources are available for research, posting videos, and connecting you with other friends and sympathetic strangers for events, gatherings, rallies, and the like. There are even resources for crowdfunding, which allows you to raise money easily via online contributions for causes and projects.

Make a Video

Online video sharing platforms like YouTube and Vimeo allow you to upload videos for free, which you can easily share via the site or copying and pasting the link and sharing it with online networks. You could make a short film that includes interviews with acquaintances and subjects familiar with the gang problem: law enforcement, psychologists, teachers, and even actual gang members and their families and friends who have dealt with the lifestyle. Another idea is to write an essay about gangs, edit stock footage, and use your words with voice-over. Remember: always obtain permission for any copyrighted materials or stick to images and audio that are in the public domain via sites like Wikimedia Commons.

Facebook, Twitter, and More: Get the Word Out

Anyone involved in organizing groups of people for important causes should consider using social media networks to get his or her message out. A Facebook account is a great tool to make announcements, create events with concrete dates and lists of attendees, and message with others, whether you are using a computer or smartphone.

Grassroots activism—empowered via online tools—has been shown to be powerful and effective in getting a message out, whatever it is. Here, anti-police-brutality protesters rally in Ferguson, Missouri, in August 2014.

Twitter offers even more targeting power for antigang campaigns with its use of hashtags. Thinking of a catchy and easy-to-replicate hashtag can even take a local gang awareness campaign and give it national and even international prominence. For example, the 2015 campaign surrounding #tothegirls encouraged women and girls to share empowering feminist messages. And after the controversial police shooting of Michael Brown in Ferguson, Missouri, in August 2014, #BlackLivesMatter was a focal point of a national effort to protest against police brutality. At the very least, a hashtag that names your community and an event can help others on Twitter share and discuss your initiative.

Consider also using the instant messaging platform WhatsApp to communicate about antigang rallies or gatherings, using its text messages, video, and other media messages. Instagram, the photo-sharing app, can have an impact through carefully selected images. Think about using photos of former gang

members who have rebuilt their lives as well as similarly inspira-
tional images or photos from successful events.

Raising Money: Crowdfunding

Even though many of these incredible tools are free or very cheap
to use, your project may require money for some of the more
ambitious things you plan to do. For example, you may want to
organize a music or talent show to raise money. But to make the
money, you need an initial cash infusion. Think about using a
crowdfunding website like Kickstarter, GoFundMe, or Indiegogo.
There are even ones that specialize in giving specifically to nonprofits and good causes, including Causes.com, CrowdRise,
and CauseVox.

Donations give people a concrete stake in your mission.
Such sites often allow both the organizers and contributors to
track if the project is meeting its financial goal. Success tends to
breed more success, as people are inspired to add more money
to what has already been donated.

One exciting thing about using the Internet and related tools
is you can easily create and amplify enthusiasm for something,
starting with just one person: yourself. Awareness can spread
exponentially, with some of your friends passing news along to
ever greater numbers of their friends, and so on.

Connecting on a Personal Level

Usually, only professionals should intervene in gang disputes—
online or off. However, this does not mean that you can't use
social media, e-mail, and various smartphone apps to send messages to friends who may be toying with joining the gang life. If

you know someone like that, the most you can do is encourage him or her in other directions, such as toward positive activities like joining clubs, playing sports, or even volunteering around the neighborhood and participating in gang-prevention activities.

These and other activities can give focus to aimless, at-risk, and troubled potential gang members, showing them there is another alternative out there. Sometimes, all it takes is one gesture to help change another person's life. Even in our hyper-connected online world, sometimes there is no substitute for the personal touch.

Glossary

CREW Another term for gang.

CROWDFUNDING Raising money online via websites dedicated to that purpose.

GANGSTA RAP A genre of rap music that arose during the 1980s that told graphic tales of urban violence.

HARDCORE Refers to gang members who are deeply involved in the gang lifestyle.

JUMPED IN A gang initiation involving being assaulted by already established members.

MUSCLE Refers to gang members whose main role in a gang is to use violence.

SCHOOL-TO-PRISON PIPELINE A phenomenon in modern schools in which certain children are disciplined in ways that strongly steer them to the penal system later in life.

STOP AND FRISK A law enforcement campaign to randomly stop and search individuals on the street; often criticized for disproportionately targeting black and brown males.

"STOP SNITCHING" An informal campaign to dissuade members of communities of color from cooperating with law enforcement.

SUPPRESSION Refers to techniques of combating the gang problem that rely largely on aggressive law enforcement.

ZERO TOLERANCE Disciplinary codes in schools that demand strict penalties for breaking rules.

Barrios Unidos
1817 Soquel Avenue
Santa Cruz, CA 95062
(831) 457-8208
Website: http://www.barriosunidos.net
Barrios Unidos—"United Neighborhoods"—is a Mexican
   American collection of grassroots community activist
   organizations that provides services and assistance to
   Latino communities throughout the United States, espe-
   cially to combat delinquency and gang violence.

Boys & Girls Clubs of America
1275 Peachtree Street NE
Atlanta, GA 30309
(404) 487-5700
E-mail: info@bgca.org
Website: http://www.bgca.org
The Boys & Girls Clubs of America aims to provide safe spaces
   in communities for children to explore activities, develop
   relationships with adult mentors, build character, and
   more with its large network of after-school programs and
   centers across the United States.

Cure Violence
1603 W. Taylor Street
Chicago, IL 60612
(312) 996-8775
Website: http://cureviolence.org

Cure Violence is an organization that approaches stopping violence as a public health issue and intervenes directly in communities to stop its spread and escalation. It has branches in US cities and is expanding throughout the world to prevent gang and sectarian violence.

Gang Resistance Education and Training (GREAT)
Institute for Intergovernmental Research
P.O. Box 12729
Tallahassee, FL 32317
(800) 726-7070
E-mail: information@great-online.org
Website: http://www.great-online.org
GREAT is a school-curriculum–based program in which law enforcement officers nationwide combat the risk factors that lead to gang involvement with an interactive curriculum.

Homeboy Industries
130 W. Bruno Street
Los Angeles, CA 90012
(323) 526-1254
E-mail: info@homeboyindustries.org
Website: http://www.homeboyindustries.org
Founded in Los Angeles in 1992, Homeboy Industries is a youth program that assists high-risk youth, including former gang members and the recently incarcerated, with job training, mentoring, legal services, education, and other assistance to help them transition out of the criminal underworld and into mainstream society.

Police Athletic League of New York
34 1/2 East 12th Street
New York, NY 10003
(212) 477-9450
Website: http://www.palnyc.org
The Police Athletic League of New York is one of the largest
networks of activities leagues, serving dozens of communities in the United States' largest city. Their programs
include athletics, arts, community volunteering, and
academic tutoring and college preparation.

Websites

Because of the changing nature of Internet links, Rosen
Publishing has developed an online list of websites related
to the subject of this book. This site is updated regularly.
Please use this link to access the list:
http://www.rosenlinks.com/ESS/Gangs

For Further Reading

Byers, Ann. *Frequently Asked Questions About Gangs and Urban Violence* (FAQ: Teen Life). New York, NY: Rosen Publishing, 2011.

Greenhaven Press. *Gangs* (Current Controversies). San Diego, CA: Greenhaven Press, 2015.

Greenhaven Press. *Juvenile Crime* (Opposing Viewpoints). San Diego, CA: Greenhaven Press, 2010.

Haerens, Margaret. *Juvenile Crime* (Global Viewpoints). San Diego, CA: Greenhaven Press, 2013.

Hess, Kären M., and Christine H. Orthmann. *Juvenile Justice*. Belmont, CA: Wadsworth Publishing, 2012.

Hiber, Amanda. *Gangs* (Issues that Concern You). San Diego, CA: Greenhaven Press, 2013.

Hile, Lori. *Gangs* (Teen Issues). Chicago, IL: Heinemann, 2012.

Levete, Sarah. Taking Action Against Gangs. New York, NY: Rosen Publishing, 2010.

MacKay, Jennifer. *Gangs* (Hot Topics). San Diego, CA: Lucent Books, 2010.

Marcovitz, Hal. *Gangs* (Essential Issues). Edina, MN: ABDO Publishing, 2010.

Parks, Peggy J. *Gangs* (Compact Research Series). San Diego, CA: Referencepoint Press, 2010.

Soliz, Adela. *Gangs* (Opposing Viewpoints). San Diego, CA: Greenhaven Press, 2009.

Bibliography

All Things Harlem. "Stop the Violence in Harlem—Gang Violence Will Get Worse Before It Gets Better." AllThingsHarlem.com video interview, 2010. Retrieved April 19, 2015 (https://vimeo.com/8231758).

Axelrod, Tal. "Gang Violence Is on the Rise, Even as Overall Violence Declines." *U.S. News* & World Report, March 6, 2015. Retrieved April 19, 2015 (http://www.usnews.com/news/articles/2015/03/06/gang-violence-is-on-the-rise-even-as-overall-violence-declines).

Berg, Nate. "The 5 U.S. Cities with the Worst Gang Violence." Citylab/The Atlantic, January 31, 2012. Retrieved April 15, 2015 (http://www.citylab.com/crime/2012/01/5-us-cities-worst-gang-violence/1095).

Bishop, Tricia. "What's in a Gang Name? Street Cred." *Baltimore Sun*, August 7, 2009. Retrieved April 15, 2015 (http://articles.baltimoresun.com/2009-08-07/news/0908070017_1_nicknames-richardson-gang).

Byrne, Ciara. "Drugs, Guns, and Selfies: Gangs on Social Media." Fast Company, February 5, 2015. Retrieved April 21, 2015 (http://www.fastcompany.com/3041479/drugs-guns-and-selfies-gangs-on-social-media).

Ebert, Roger. "*The Interrupters*: Movie Review." Rogerebert.com, August 10, 2011. Retrieved April 20, 2015 (http://www.rogerebert.com/reviews/the-interrupters-2011).

Gorner, Jeremy. "Chicago Violence Continues to Outpace NYC and LA." *Chicago Tribune*, July 1, 2014. Retrieved April 15, 2015 (http://www.chicagotribune.com/news

/ct-chicago-police-shootings-homicide-met
-20140701-story.html).

Hamilton, Brad. "Rise of the Girl Gangs." *New York Post*,
December 4, 2011. Retrieved April 14, 2015 (http://nypost
.com/2011/12/04/rise-of-the-girl-gangs).

Harmann, Peter. "Nicknames Among Gang Members Become
More Sinister." Baltimore Sun, July 13, 2010. Retrieved
April 7, 2015 (http://articles.baltimoresun.com/2010-07-13
/news/bs-md-hermann-nicknames-crime-20100713_1
_nicknames-gang-members-tattooed).

Justice.gov. "Drugs and Gangs—Fast Facts." Department of
Justice website, July 1, 2009. Retrieved April 20, 2015
(http://www.justice.gov/archive/ndic/pubs11/13157).

National Gang Center. "Frequently Asked Questions About
Gangs." Retrieved April 20, 2015 (http://www
.nationalgangcenter.gov/about/FAQ).

Nickeas, Peter. "Fourth of July Weekend Toll: 82 Shot, 14 of
Them Fatally, in Chicago." *Chicago Tribune*, July 7, 2014.
Retrieved April 15, 2015 (http://articles.chicagotribune
.com/2014-07-07/news/chi-fourth-of-july-toll-82-shot-14
-of-them-fatally-in-chicago-20140707_1_south-chicago
-east-garfield-park-west-englewood).

Norfleet, Nicole. "St. Paul Police and Partners Start New
Gang Intervention Program." *Star Tribune*, October 30,
2013. Retrieved April 21, 2015 (http://www.startribune
.com/local/east/229805081.html).

O'Reilly, Andre. "Gang Warfare on Streets of Chicago Fueled
by Sinaloa Cartel Heroin." *Fox News Latino*, February 5,
2015. Retrieved April 10, 2015 (http://latino.foxnews.com
/latino/news/2015/02/05/gang-warfare-on-streets-chicago
-fueled-by-sinaloa-cartel-heroin).

PBS.org. "The Interrupters." *Frontline*, February 14, 2012. Retrieved April 10, 2015 (http://www.pbs.org/wgbh /pages/frontline/interrupters).

Popper, Ben. "How the NYPD Is Using Social Media to Put Harlem Teens Behind Bars." *The Verge*, December 10, 2014. Retrieved April 20, 2015 (http://www.theverge .com/2014/12/10/7341077/nypd-harlem-crews-social -media-rikers-prison).

Quinones, Sam. "The End of Gangs." *Pacific Standard*, December 29, 2014. Retrieved April 22, 2015 (http://www .psmag.com/politics-and-law/the-end-of-gangs-los -angeles-southern-california-epidemic-crime-95498).

Weichselbaum, Simone. "Gangs in New York Talk Twitter: Use Tweets to Trash-talk Rivals, Plan Fights." *New York Daily* News, November 28, 2009. Retrieved April 20, 2015 (http://www.nydailynews.com/news/crime/gangs-new -york-talk-twitter-tweets-trash-talk-rivals-plan-fights -article-1.414083).

Index

A

Aggression Replacement Training (ART), 41

B

Boys & Girls Clubs of America, 39
bullying, 6, 27, 44–47

C

CeaseFire, 40
clothes, 9–10
colors, gang, 9–10, 25
crowdfunding, 49, 52
cyberbullying, 6, 44–45

D

disrespect and respect, 14, 15, 22
drug dealing, 4, 11, 14, 20, 33

F

friends, choosing wisely, 26–27

G

Gang Resistance and Education and Training (GREAT), 39
gangs and gang violence
avoiding and dealing with, 26–33, 47
characteristics of, 8–9
combating, 6, 34–43, 46–53
defined, 7
effects of on non-gang members, 16–17
increase in, 4, 34
informing on, 29
joining, 31–33
online presence, 6, 44–45, 46–47
reasons for violence, 14
standing up to, 29, 45
telltale signs of members, 9, 25
what gangs do, 13–15
where gangs form, 4, 6, 13, 18
why people join gangs, 17–22
gang signs, 13, 25
gangsta rap, 42–43
girls, and gangs, 19, 23–24
graffiti, 15, 16

H

heroin, 4, 11

I

initiation, 31–32
Interrupters, The, 40

J

James, Steve, 40

L

Latino gangs, 10
legal counsel, 30

M

mentors, 41

N

National Association of Police
    Athletics/Activities Leagues
    (PAL), 39
National Gang Center, 4, 8, 14, 23

O

organized crime, 7
organizing online, 48–53

P

Perfect Peace Ministry Youth
    Outreach, 47–48
police, and gangs, 34–37, 39
pop culture, and glorification of
    gangs, 42–43
protecting yourself, 30

S

school-to-prison pipeline, 36–37
self-defense, 31
social pressure, 21–22
social services, 38, 41
suppression of gangs, 35–36, 37–38

T

tattoos, 9, 11–12, 25

V

violence, avoiding, 30
Violence Intervention and
    Prevention (VIP) project, 38

W

weapons, 11, 20–21, 31
Williams, Vernon, 46–47

Z

zero tolerance policies, 37–38

About the Author

Philip Wolny is a writer and editor raised in Queens, New York City. He attended Stuyvesant High School at the end of the 1980s, one of the city's most violent eras. He fortunately escaped mostly unscathed. He has written other cautionary nonfiction titles for Rosen Publishing targeted at teens, including *I Have an STD. Now What?* (Teen Life 411) and *The Truth About Heroin* (Drugs & Consequences).

Photo Credits

Cover © iStockphoto.com/monkeybusinessimages; p. 5 Mauro Rodrigues/Shutterstock.com; pp.8, 19, 32 Monkey Business Images/Shutterstock.com; pp. 10, 17 Robert Nickelsberg/Getty Images; p. 12 ES James/Shutterstock.com; p. 14 Binkski/Shutterstock.com; p. 21 vidguten/Shutterstock.com; p. 24 Peter Kim/Shutterstock.com; p. 27 Tad Denson/Shutterstock.com; p. 28 GlebStock/Shutterstock.com; p. 35 Photofusion/Universal Images Group/Getty Images; p. 37 sakhorn/Shutterstock.com; p. 42 lev radin/Shutterstock.com; p. 45 SpeedKingz/Shutterstock.com; p. 48 Samuel Borges Photography/Shutterstock.com; pp. 50-51 Michael B. Thomas/Getty Images; back cover and interior pages background pattern ONiONA/Shutterstock.com

Designer: Nicole Russo; Editor: Tracey Baptiste